GUTS
OUR DIGESTIVE SYSTEM

S E Y M O U R S I M O N

Updated Edition

HARPER
An Imprint of HarperCollinsPublishers

To my literary agent, Wendy Schmalz, who knows the other meaning of the word "guts."

Special thanks to Robert Byrne

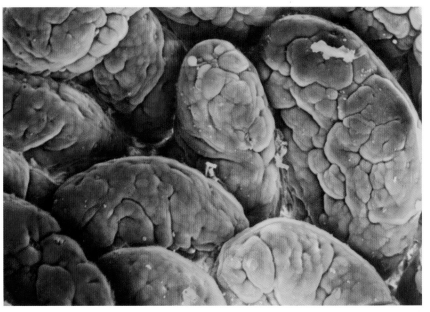

Photo and Illustration Credits

Page 2: © Prof Cinti & V. Gremet / Science Source; page 4: © Vero/Carlo/ PhotoResearchers; page 6: © Ted Kinsman / Science Source; page 7: © BSIP / UIG; page 8: © Steve Gschmeissner / Science Source; page 11: © L. Bassett / Visuals Unlimited; page 12: © Biophoto Associates / Science Source; page 13: © SIU / Visuals Unlimited; page 14: © David M. Martin, M.D. / Science Photo Library; page 15: © Andy Crump / Science Source; page 17: © Alfred Pasieka / Science Photo Library; page 18: © Susumu Nishinaga / Science Source; page 20: © SIU / Visuals Unlimited; page 21: © Stocktrek Images / Science Source; page 22: © Thomas Deerinck, NCMIR / Science Source; page 25: © SPL / Science Source; page 26: © Gastrolab / Science Source; page 27: © SPL / Science Source; page 29: © Carol and Mike Werner / Science Source; page 30: © MedicalRF / Visuals Unlimited

Library of Congress Control Number: 2018939988
ISBN 978-0-06-247042-3 (trade bdg.) — ISBN 978-0-06-247041-6 (pbk.)

18 19 20 21 22 SCP 10 9 8 7 6 5 4 3 2 1
❖
Revised edition, 2019

Author's Note

From a young age, I was interested in animals, space, my surroundings—all the natural sciences. When I was a teenager, I became the president of a nationwide junior astronomy club with a thousand members. After college, I became a classroom teacher for nearly twenty-five years while also writing articles and books for children on science and nature even before I became a full-time writer. My experience as a teacher gives me the ability to understand how to reach my young readers and get them interested in the world around us.

I've written more than 300 books, and I've thought a lot about different ways to encourage interest in the natural world, as well as how to show the joys of nonfiction. When I write, I use comparisons to help explain unfamiliar ideas, complex concepts, and impossibly large numbers. I try to engage your senses and imagination to set the scene and to make science fun. For example, in *Penguins*, I emphasize the playful nature of these creatures on the very first page by mentioning how penguins excel at swimming and diving. I use strong verbs to enhance understanding. I make use of descriptive detail and ask questions that anticipate what you may be thinking (sometimes right at the start of the book).

Many of my books are photo-essays, which use extraordinary photographs to amplify and expand the text, creating different and engaging ways of exploring nonfiction. You'll also find a glossary, an index, and website and research recommendations in most of my books, which make them ideal for enhancing your reading and learning experience. As William Blake wrote in his poem, I want my readers "to see a world in a grain of sand, / And a heaven in a wild flower, / Hold infinity in the palm of your hand, / And eternity in an hour."

Seymour Simon

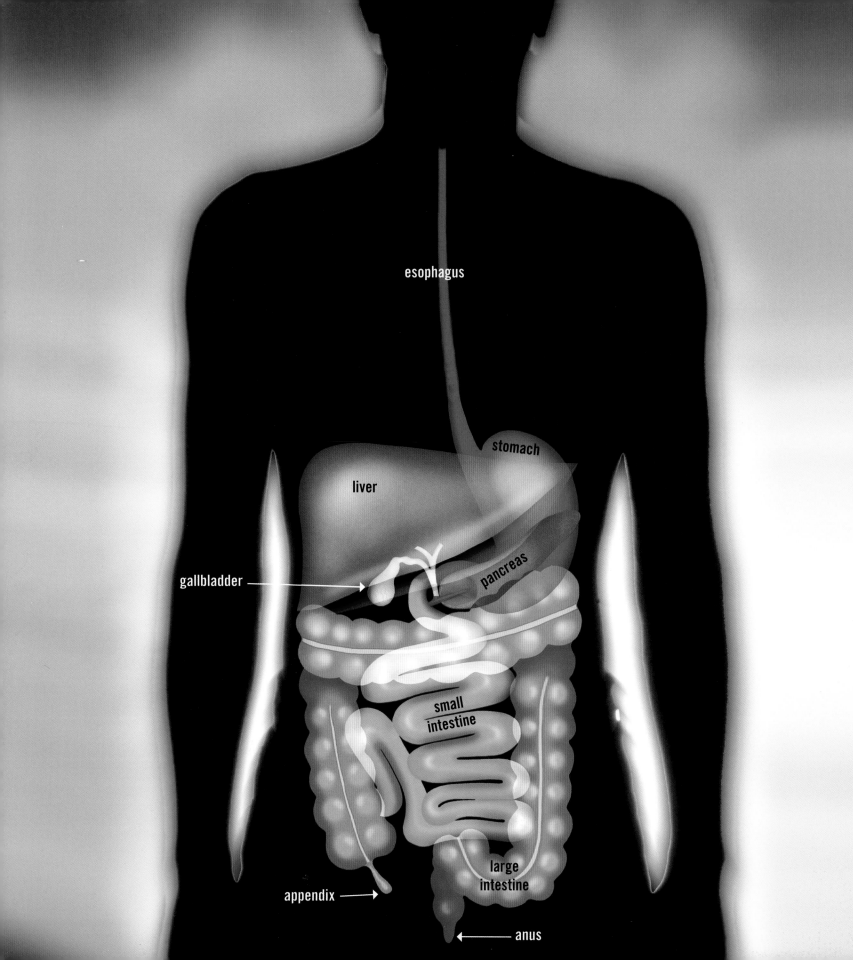

You probably eat three meals and several snacks a day. That adds up to hundreds of pounds of food in a year. The digestive system turns the truckload of sandwiches, milk, salads, and pizzas that you eat each year into the energy and the nutrients that your body needs.

Digestion takes place in a long tube inside the body called the digestive tract, or gut. The digestive tract begins in the mouth and runs through the **esophagus**, the stomach, and the small and large intestines. Finally the body gets rid of undigested food waste through the anus. Food takes about twenty to forty hours to travel through your body.

Baby tooth with cavity and cracks.

The beginning of digestion happens in our mouths. Your teeth are the hardest parts of your body. They have to be. You use your teeth to bite, tear, chop, and grind the food you eat into smaller pieces that are easier to swallow and digest.

The chisel-shaped front teeth are called incisors. They're used to slice off chunks of food. The pointed canine teeth just beside the incisors are good for ripping and tearing at food. The flat-topped teeth behind the canines are the premolars and the molars. Molars are used for chewing and grinding food down into a pulp.

Some animals, such as dogs and cats, just bolt down food in large chunks. But people need to chew their food slowly so that it can be swallowed and digested. First, taste buds in your tongue check the food in your mouth to make sure you want to eat it. Then your lips and cheeks and tongue push the food back toward the molars.

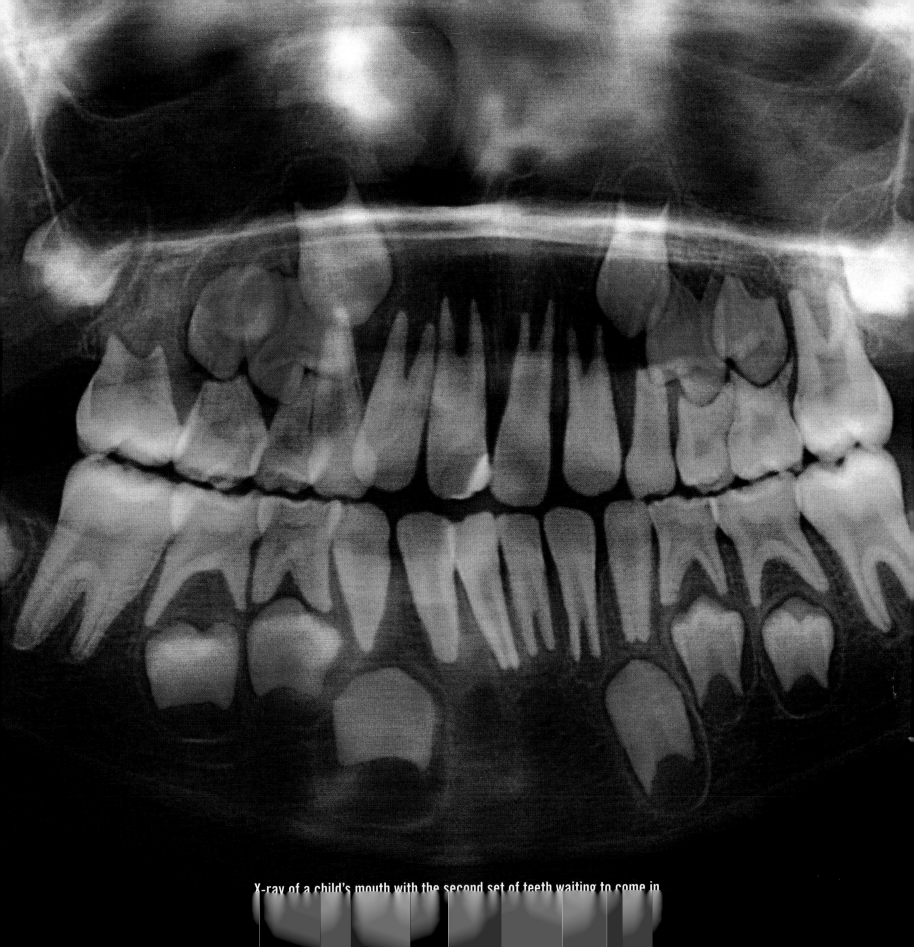

X-ray of a child's mouth with the second set of teeth waiting to come in.

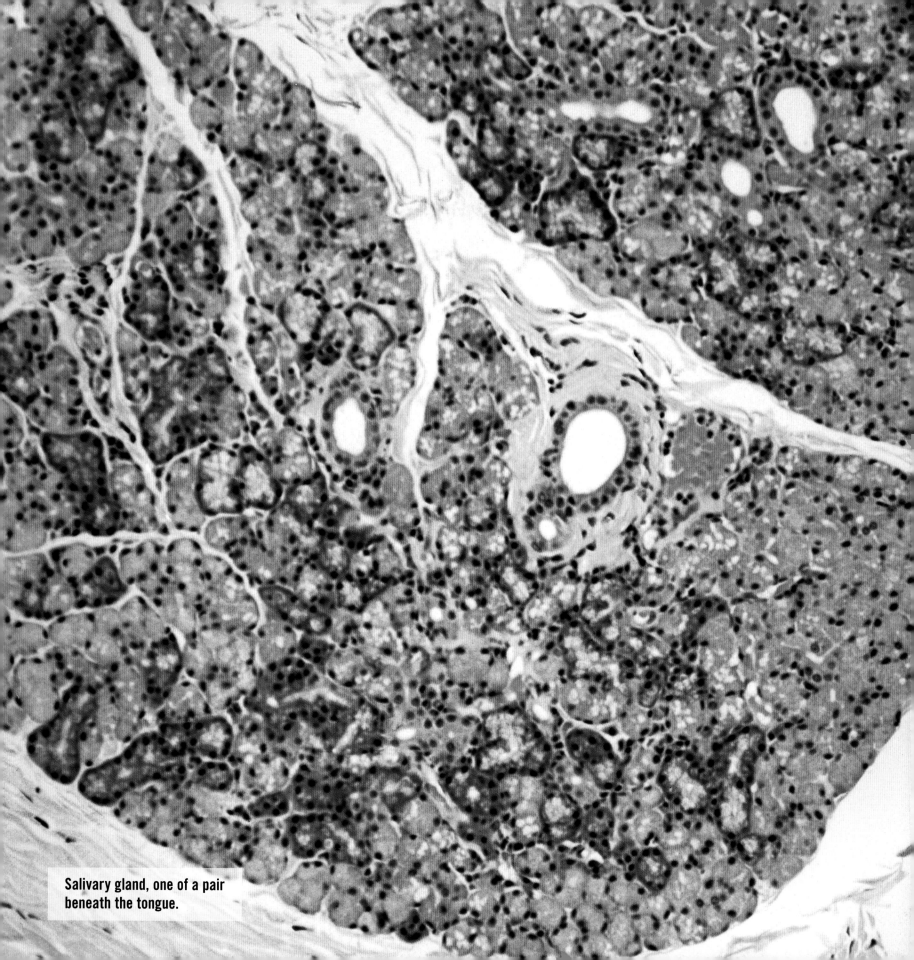

Salivary gland, one of a pair beneath the tongue.

The act of chewing crushes and mashes food together with watery saliva, or spit. As soon as you smell the odor of a food you like, your mouth begins to water, or salivate. Saliva comes from three pairs of salivary glands—at the back of the mouth, under the tongue, and under the sides of the lower jaw. Saliva contains substances called **enzymes**, which help break down food into nutrients that the body can use. There are thousands of digestive enzymes throughout the human digestive system. For example, one enzyme in saliva called amylase starts the breakdown of larger molecules of starch into smaller, simpler molecules of sugar. You can see this for yourself by chewing on a piece of bread and letting it stay in your mouth. Bread is a starchy food without much of a taste. But after a few minutes, the chewed bread will begin to taste sweet. Now try chewing on a piece of nonstarchy food such as a peanut or a piece of cheese. It won't taste sweet no matter how long you keep it in your mouth.

The wet lump of chewed food in your mouth is called a **bolus**. Your tongue presses the bolus backward toward your throat, and you swallow. As soon as you swallow, digestion goes on automatically.

After you swallow, food travels through a tube called the esophagus that leads down from the back of your throat to your stomach. The top of the esophagus also opens into your nose. But you certainly don't want food to go up your nose. When you swallow, a flap called the soft palate blocks off the opening to your nasal canal, preventing food from coming out of your nose. Lower down, the esophagus opens into a tube that takes air into your lungs. A trapdoor called the **epiglottis** closes off this opening and prevents food from getting down into your lungs.

When you swallow food, it doesn't just fall into your stomach. In fact, you can eat standing on your head (don't try it, though; you might choke) and still get food to your stomach. Food is pushed along by two sets of muscles that line the esophagus. The muscles tighten and relax, pushing food along the tube—similar to you squeezing a tube of toothpaste. This movement is called **peristalsis**. Thick, slimy mucus coats the inside of the gut and makes it easier for food to slip along.

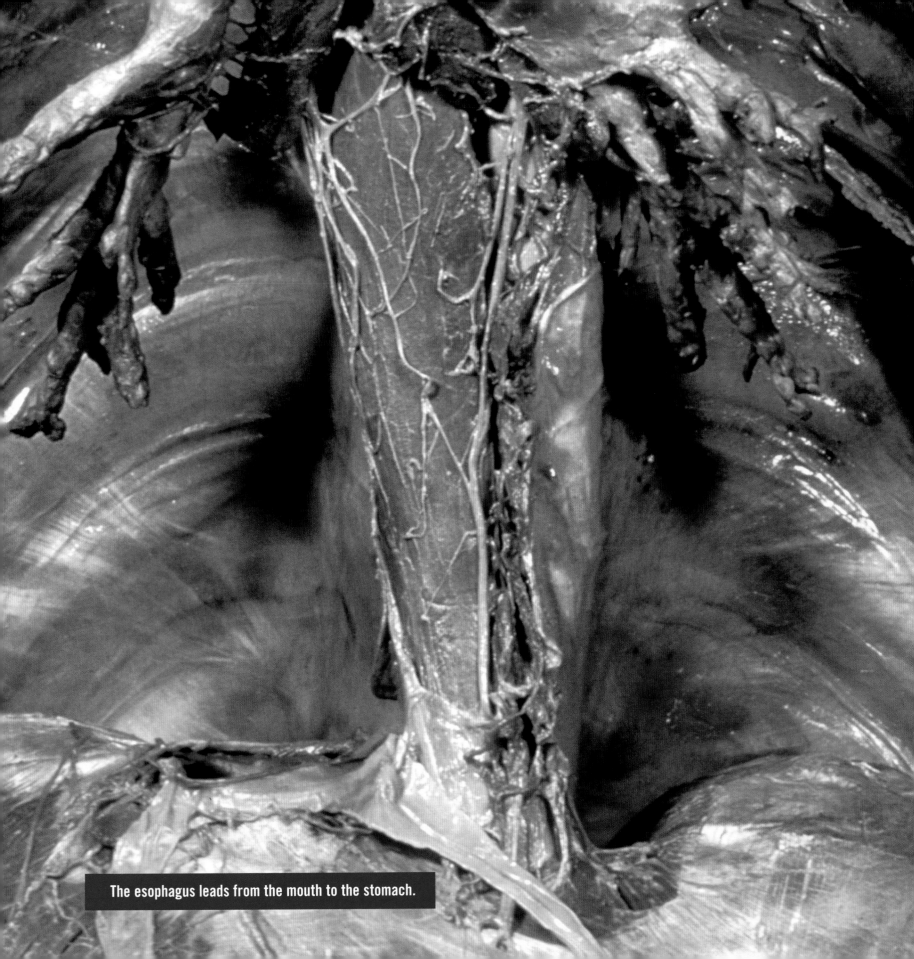

The esophagus leads from the mouth to the stomach.

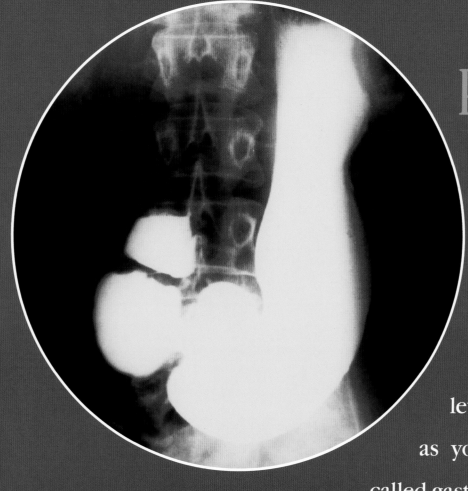

Point to your stomach. Surprise! It's not behind your belly button but higher up, tucked just beneath the left side of your rib cage. An empty stomach is shaped like the letter *J*, and it's about as big as your fist. Deep, soft folds called gastric rugae line the inside of your stomach. After you eat a meal, the folds flatten out and your stomach swells up. It can get as big as a boxing glove.

Once the chewed-up food enters the stomach, the food is mixed with a fluid called gastric, or stomach, juice. Millions of tiny pits in the wall of the stomach contain glands that produce

gastric juice. The stomach produces about eight cups of gastric juice every day. Gastric juice is made up of different substances that help to digest food. One of these, hydrochloric acid, helps to soften food. The acid bath also helps to kill any germs in food. Digestive enzymes and watery mucus make up the rest of gastric juice.

Hydrochloric acid is so powerful that it could burn a hole in clothing or dissolve an iron nail. So why doesn't it burn holes in the wall of your stomach? The reason is that it is lined with a coating of protective mucus. Even so, the mucus cells wear out quickly and are replaced. Every three or four days, you have an entirely new stomach lining.

The soupy mixture of food and gastric juices in your stomach is called **chyme**. When the chyme is liquid enough, peristalsis moves the food downward to the end of the stomach. Sometimes peristaltic waves help to get rid of harmful food that isn't properly digested because you are sick or because the food is bad. The waves push food upward through the esophagus and out through your mouth as vomit! In the vomit, you can see what food looks like in your stomach. Not a pretty sight!

At the bottom of the stomach is a ring of muscles called the **pyloric sphincter**. When food first enters the stomach, the sphincter is closed so tightly that nothing can leave. Three sets of powerful muscles make up most of the stomach wall. The muscles squeeze and tighten about three times a minute, mixing and churning the food inside. As food is

Pyloric sphincter seen through a tiny camera known as a "pill camera."

digested, the muscles start to relax. With each peristaltic wave, a squirt of chyme passes into the small intestine.

Foods stay in the stomach for different amounts of time. Water passes through very quickly. Meals made up mostly of breads or pasta pass through in an hour or so. But greasy, fatty foods such as double cheeseburgers and fries stay in the stomach for three to four hours or longer.

This color-enhanced photo of the pyloric sphincter (opposite page) was taken inside the stomach of a living person by a tiny wireless camera called an **endoscope** capsule or pill camera. The camera is inside a vitamin-sized capsule that is swallowed. As it travels through your digestive tract, the camera takes thousands of pictures so that a doctor can consult.

The small intestine is anything but small. In fact, the small intestine is the biggest and most important part of the digestive system. It's only called "small" because it is narrower than the large intestine. The small intestine is about an inch thick tube that gets to be about twenty feet long. The tube is all folded up and fits inside the midsection of your body below the rib cage. Food stays in the small intestine for one to six hours. Most digestion happens as food travels through the twists and turns of the small intestine.

The small intestine is made up of three sections that work in different ways. Chyme is squeezed from the stomach into the first section, called the **duodenum**. The duodenum is shaped like the letter *C* and is about a foot long. The second section, called the **jejunum**, is about eight feet long. The main work of digestion takes place in the first two sections of the small intestine.

The third and longest section is called the **ileum**. This is where food nutrients leave the digestive system and are absorbed into the body. By the time food passes out of the small intestine and into the large intestine, mostly waste matter is left.

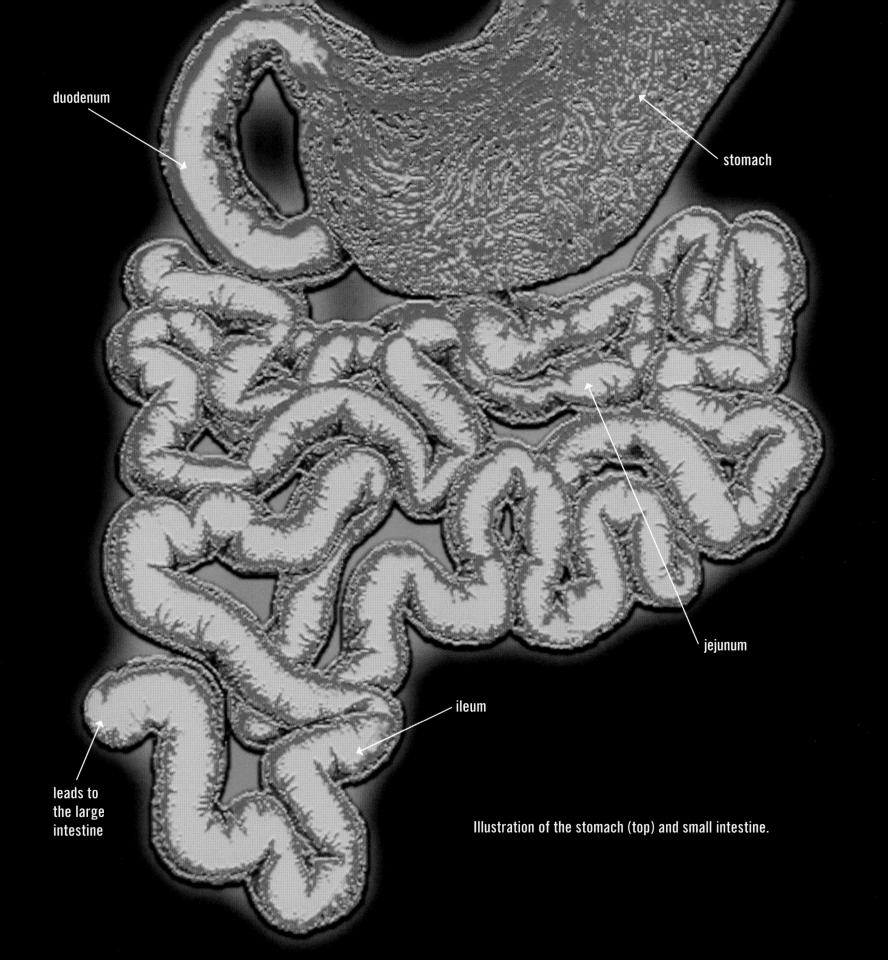

duodenum

stomach

jejunum

ileum

leads to
the large
intestine

Illustration of the stomach (top) and small intestine.

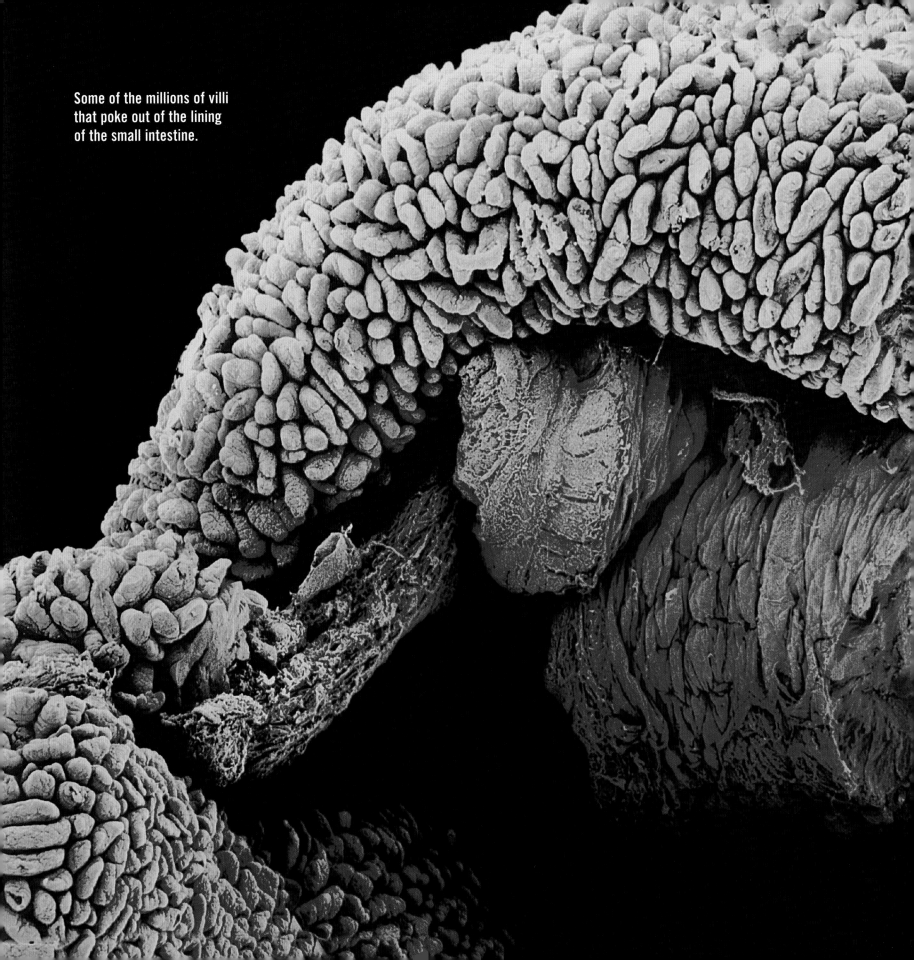

Some of the millions of villi that poke out of the lining of the small intestine.

The inner lining of the small intestine is about twenty-seven hundred square feet, 135 times greater than the area your skin covers and almost the size of a tennis court. That seems like a huge amount of space to fit inside your body! The greater the exposed wall in the small intestine, the more absorption can take place. One of the ways this is possible is because the inside wall is covered with millions of tiny projections called **villi**. The villi are covered with even tinier ones known as microvilli. All together, the folds, villi, and microvilli make the inside surface of the small intestine about six hundred times greater than if it were smooth.

Villi contain a network of tiny blood vessels called **capillaries**. Digested proteins and sugars pass through the walls of the villi and through the thin capillary walls into the blood. Villi also contain tiny tubes called **lacteals**. Digested fat nutrients pass into the lacteals that finally connect with the blood. The villi are always bending and waving like a field of wheat in the wind. The movements help to keep the blood flowing through the capillaries into the bloodstream.

When chyme squirts in from the stomach, cells in the lining of the small intestine start to make intestinal juice, which contains enzymes that help in digesting food nutrients such as **proteins**, **carbohydrates**, and **fats**. Intestinal juice also contains mucus that coats and helps to protect the lining to the small intestine.

The small intestine would be unable to digest food without two other body organs: the pancreas and the liver. The pancreas is about six inches long and looks like a flat fish lying behind the stomach. It produces pancreatic juice, a mixture of digestive enzymes, along with a chemical that neutralizes stomach acid.

The liver is the largest internal organ of the body, weighing about three or four pounds. It lies next to the stomach on the right side of your body, just below the rib cage. The liver makes bile, a substance that breaks down globs of fat into tiny droplets that are easier to digest. The bile is stored in a small organ called the gallbladder. The liver and the pancreas each have tubes that join together, sharing a common opening into the duodenum.

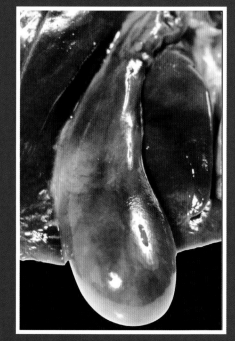

The gallbladder (foreground) and red tissue of the liver behind it.

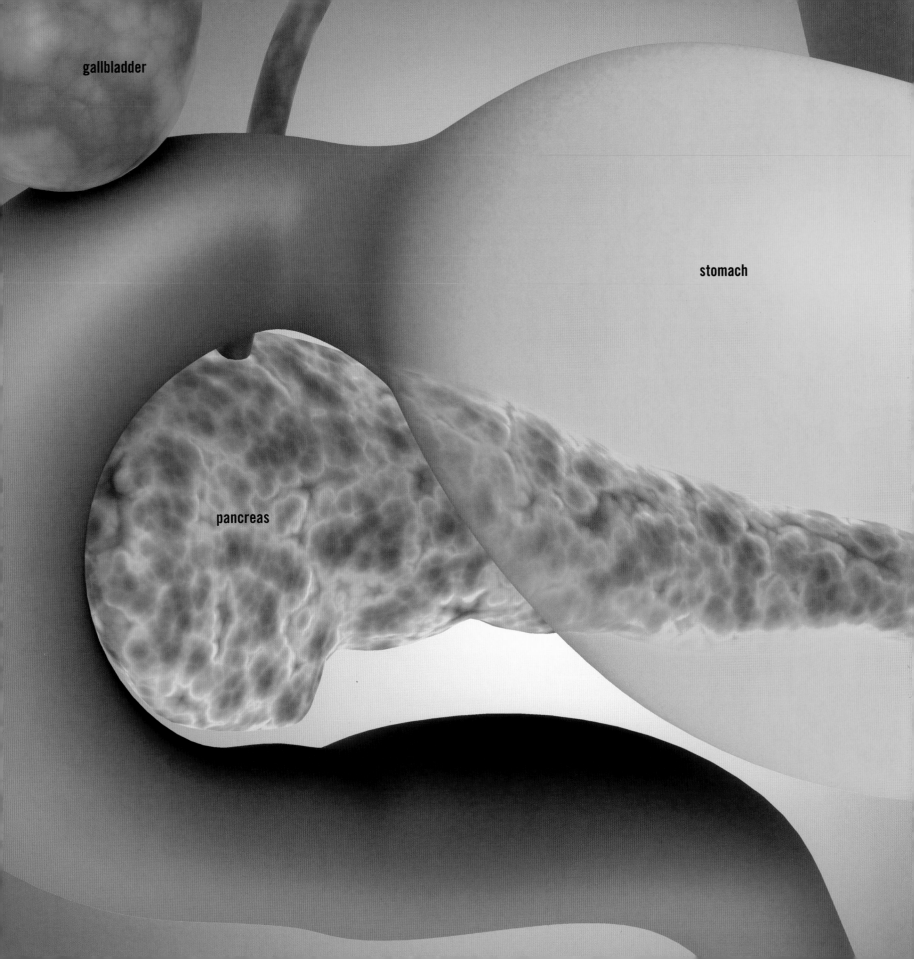

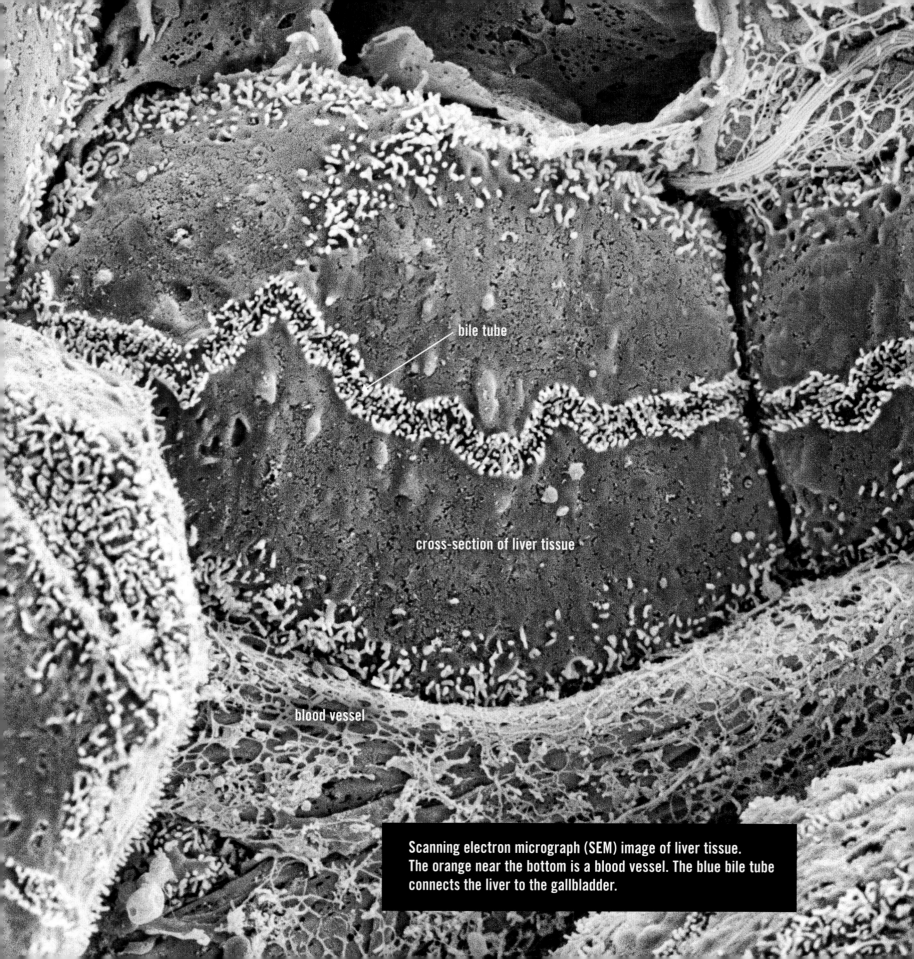

bile tube

cross-section of liver tissue

blood vessel

Scanning electron micrograph (SEM) image of liver tissue.
The orange near the bottom is a blood vessel. The blue bile tube
connects the liver to the gallbladder.

The pancreas and the liver have other important jobs. The pancreas is really two organs in one. First, it makes pancreatic juice that pours into the small intestine and helps digest foods. The pancreas also makes chemicals called **hormones** that go into the bloodstream. Hormones help regulate body functions such as energy use and growth.

Insulin is a hormone that is made by the pancreas. Insulin controls how much sugar the body uses for energy for immediate use and how much is stored for future use. If the pancreas does not produce enough insulin, a person may develop diabetes. Diabetes is a disease in which the sugar level in the blood is not controlled.

The liver is the body's chemical factory, not only producing bile but also doing hundreds of other jobs in the body. The liver stores sugar in one chemical form and then changes the sugar into another form when the body needs energy. It stores vitamins and iron, filters the blood, and gets rid of poisons and wastes. It also makes **cholesterol** and proteins needed for blood clotting. The liver has an amazing ability to repair itself. Even if most of it is injured, the small piece remaining can grow back to a full-size organ.

The large intestine is the last part of the gut. It's much smaller than the small intestine, about five to six feet long. But it's called the large intestine because it's two to three inches wide, more than twice as wide as the small intestine.

The first part of the large intestine is the colon. The small intestine joins the colon at the lower right side of your midsection. The colon goes up the right side, bends sideways below your rib cage, and then turns downward and back to connect with your rectum. The rectum, a straight, five-inch-long tube, leads to the anus, an opening to the outside. A powerful ring of muscles holds the end of the rectum closed.

A lot of water is needed to move food through the gut and help digestion. But the body does not lose the water. As the remains of the food travel through the large intestine, most of the water, along with minerals and vitamins, is absorbed back into the body.

Digested food spends five to ten hours in the large intestine and turns into masses called feces. Feces contain water, undigested food material, dead body cells, and bacteria. Feces are expelled through the anus. This is called defecation, the final part of digestion.

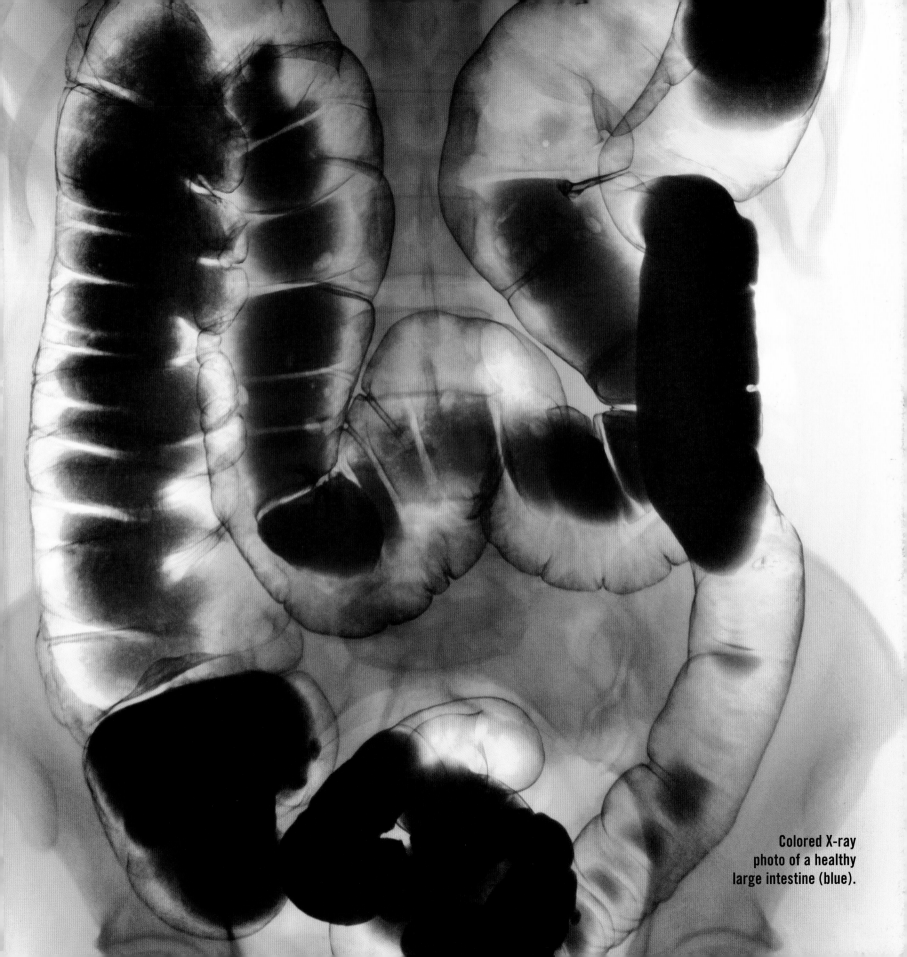

Colored X-ray photo of a healthy large intestine (blue).

The lining of the large intestine (right) is much smoother than the lining of the small intestine. It doesn't have villi, but it does have small glands that produce mucus. The inside of the large intestine is covered with cells to absorb water.

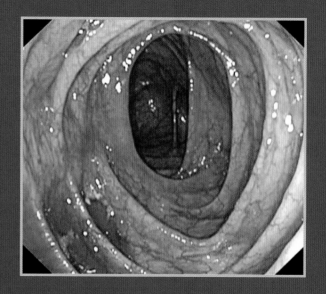

There are more bacteria in the large intestine than in any other part of the body. The bacteria here are typically not harmful, though. They break down waste, and some bacteria even make vitamins that the body can use. But bacteria working on waste produce gas bubbles. Sometimes the gas makes embarrassing noises or produces bad smells when it is expelled.

One small organ attached to the digestive system is the appendix. Scientists recently discovered that it is a safe place to store good bacteria used to help digest food. It is connected to the first part of the large intestine just where it joins the small intestine. But the appendix may cause trouble in people when it gets infected so badly that it has to be removed.

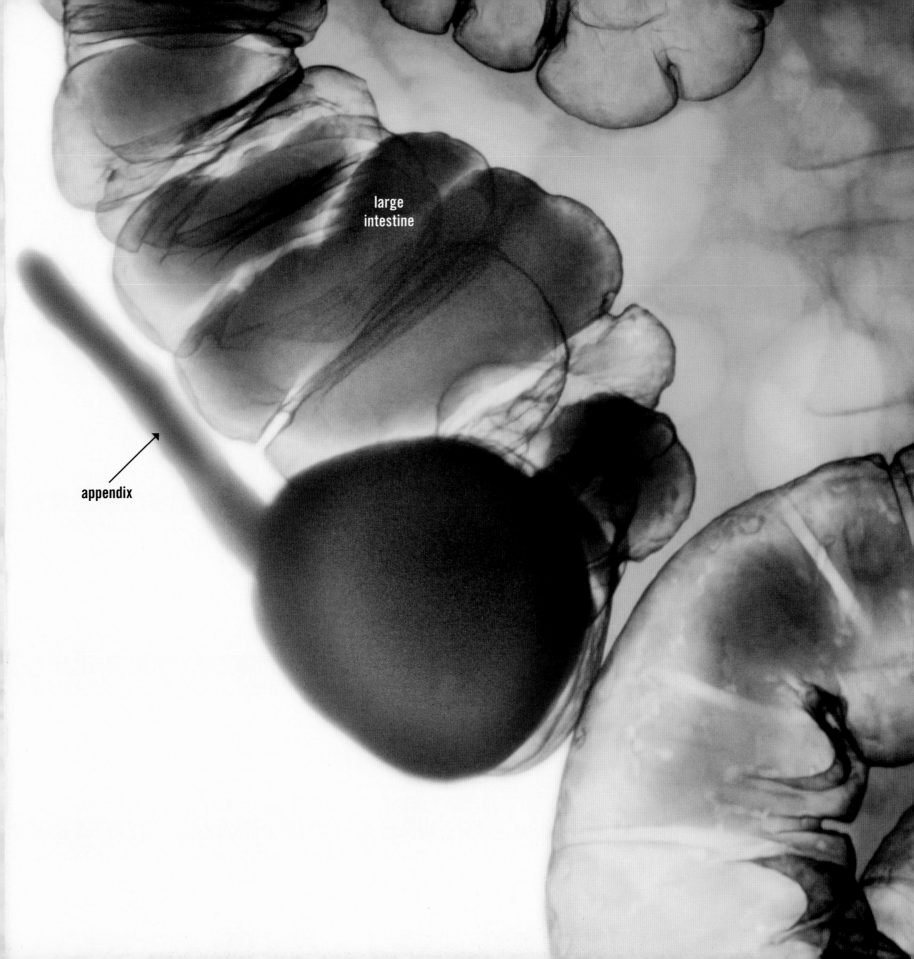

large
intestine

appendix

Most of the time the digestive system works just fine. But sometimes things can go wrong. You can get an upset stomach because you've eaten something that has spoiled. Harmful bacteria or viruses can also cause an upset stomach. Diarrhea is when you have watery feces and need to use the toilet often. Constipation is when you have hard feces that are difficult to get out. Heartburn and indigestion are sometimes caused by eating too quickly and not relaxing while you eat. They can also be caused by certain foods to which you have an allergy.

Eating the right kinds of food in the right amounts, neither too much nor too little, can prevent many digestive problems. A healthy food plate consists of a large serving of vegetables, equal portions of fruits, grains, and proteins, and a small serving of milk or other dairy products.

If you ever think that there is something wrong with your digestion, you should talk to a parent, teacher, school nurse, or doctor. Regular checkups are important for keeping healthy.

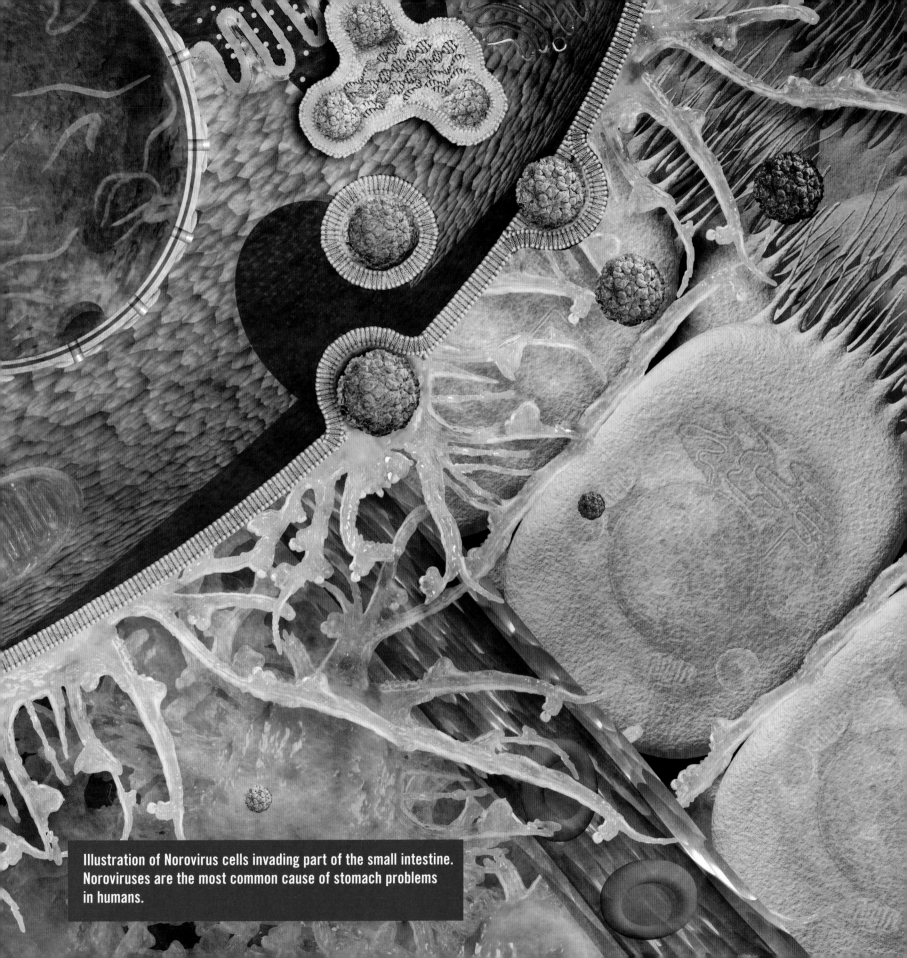

Illustration of Norovirus cells invading part of the small intestine. Noroviruses are the most common cause of stomach problems in humans.

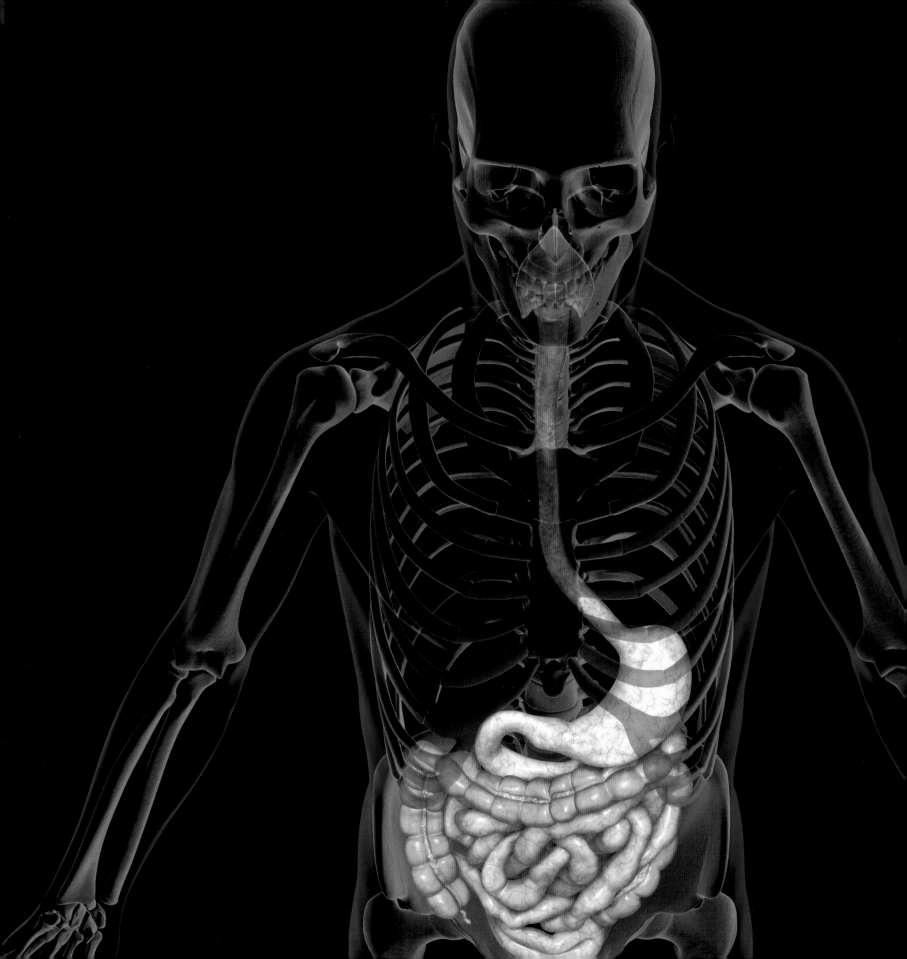

You are what you eat. That doesn't mean that if you eat a carrot, you will have a carrot growing out of your ear. The food that you eat travels from your mouth to your esophagus, then to your stomach and to your small intestine, and finally to your large intestine and out of your body. Along the way, the food is broken down into substances that your body can use.

A well-balanced diet is needed to be healthy. For young people, a balanced diet provides the vitamins, minerals, proteins, and other nutrients needed to develop strong bones, grow well, and be active and alert. Without a good diet, your body is more prone to disease, infection, tiredness, and poor performance. Truly you are made of the fruits and vegetables, cereals and breads, dairy products, meat, and fish that are digested in their journey through your gut.

GLOSSARY

Bolus—The small ball of food and saliva that forms in the mouth just before swallowing.

Capillaries—Tiny vessels that carry blood from small arteries to small veins.

Carbohydrates—A substance made up of carbon, hydrogen, and oxygen.

Cholesterol—A chemical found in most animal tissues and in many foods, such as egg yolks and meats.

Chyme—A pulpy fluid of gastric juices and partly digested food that passes from the stomach to the small intestine.

Duodenum—The upper, or first, part of the small intestine.

Endoscope—An instrument that can be put inside the body to give a view of the internal parts.

Enzymes—Complex substances found in living things that control chemical actions without being changed themselves. An average cell in the human body contains about three thousand different enzymes.

Epiglottis—A flap of tissue behind the tongue that covers the windpipe during swallowing, which prevents water and food from getting into the lungs.

Esophagus—The gullet, or tube, through which food passes from the mouth to the stomach.

Fats—Greasy substances found in the tissues of many animals and plants. Fats are also in foods such as butter, oil, and margarine.

Gastric juice—The thin, acidic digestive fluid that is made by various glands in the stomach to help in food digestion. It contains hydrochloric acid and several enzymes, including pepsin and rennin.

Hormones—Chemical substances found in humans and other animals that affect growth, behavior, and many other body functions.

Ileum—The third and last part of the small intestine between the jejunum and the large intestine.

Jejunum—The middle part of the small intestine between the duodenum and the ileum.

Lacteals—The lymph vessels of the small intestine that absorb digested fats.

Peristalsis—Wavelike and involuntary muscle movement in the alimentary canal that cause food to be mixed and moved onward through the digestive tract.

Proteins—A group of complex organic substances found in all living things. Proteins contain carbon, hydrogen, oxygen, nitrogen, and usually sulfur. They make up large molecules called polypeptides.

Pyloric sphincter—A band of smooth muscle at the junction between the stomach and the small intestine. It acts as a valve to control the flow of partially digested food.

Villi—Tiny hairlike projections that cover the wall of the small intestine causing digested foods to be absorbed more quickly and easily into the body.

INDEX

READ MORE ABOUT IT

Seymour Simon's website
www.seymoursimon.com

Women's and Children's Health Network
**www.cyh.com/HealthTopics/HealthTopicDetailsKids.
aspx?id=2727&np=152&p=335**

Kids Health
www.kidshealth.org/en/kids/digestive-system.html

National Geographic Kids
**www.natgeokids.com/uk/discover/science/general-science/
digestive-system**